Roman Catholicism

The Testimony of
History and Scripture

Peter Slomski

Contents

An Explanation and a Plea

This study was originally prepared for the weekly Bible study of the church I attend in Halifax, England. It's purpose was to inform Christians of the history and the beliefs of the Roman Catholic Church and in so doing to warn of error. It subsequently 'crossed' the Irish Sea and was first serialised in *Knock News*, a church magazine in Belfast, Northern Ireland and then in the Evangelical Protestant Society's quarterly, *The Ulster Bulwark*.

Perhaps you are not what may be referred to as a 'Protestant' or 'Evangelical', but rather a Roman Catholic. You may read this study and feel aggrieved at what is said about the Roman Catholic Church. If this is the case, I would have one plea: that you would please consider carefully what is written and search history's records and the Word of God to see if it is not so.

I write as one who was brought up in a (Polish) Roman Catholic home and who attended the mass and confession regularly. In my short lifetime I have known my uncle, grandmother and father die as Roman Catholics and die with what appeared to be no assurance of peace. They clung on to the Roman Catholic faith but at the expense of true peace.

But Christ has given us a certain hope and peace. He told His disciples: *"Let not your heart be troubled: ye believe in God, believe also in me...I go to prepare a place for you"*. If it depended on our good works and the sacraments we could never be sure of heaven. Salvation, however, can be certain, because Christ and His work is complete and sure. From the cross He said. *"It is finished"*. It is *trusting in Him alone and His finished work*, not in the church or in what we can do, that we can find the peace of sins forgiven and the assurance of heaven.

I hope that you too may know that sure peace with God.

Peter Slomski
Halifax, England
January 2006

Part 1

Roman
Catholic
History

Serious Questions

Do the following mean anything to you?

- National Evangelical Anglican Congress – NEAC 2 (1977) and NEAC 3 (1988),

- Anglican-Roman Catholic International Commission, or better known as ARCIC I (1982) and ARCIC II (1987),

- Evangelicals and Catholics Together: The Christian Mission in the Third Millennium – ECT (1994) and ECT II: The Gift of Salvation (1997),

- The World Lutheran Federation and the Catholic Church Joint Declaration on the Doctrine of Justification (1999),

- "Mary: Hope and Grace in Christ" document (2005).

These are all attempts to bring the Roman Catholic (RC) Church and Protestant churches together and demonstrate that the differences are not that great.

What about the following Christian organisations: the Billy Graham Association, Campus Crusade, Focus on the Family, Promise Keepers, Scripture Gift Mission, Wycliffe Bible Translators, and YWAM? These are organisations which rather than try to evangelise RCs are working together with RCs.

What about the following respected Christian leaders: Bill Bright, Chuck Colson, Nicky Gumbel, Billy Graham, J.I. Packer, Pat Robertson and John Stott?[1] These and others have furthered the belief that although there are differences between RCs and Evangelicals, they are all brothers and sisters in Christ.

Was the Reformation a mistake ... Were Christians wrong in dying for their faith at the hands of Rome...?

Are they right? Was the Reformation a mistake, when Martin Luther made his stand and protested in the 16th century against RC doctrine? Were Christians wrong in dying for their faith at the hands of Rome rather than agree with its teachings? Perhaps Rome has changed? Should we all join hands and be one 'happy family'?

We will see that both history and Scripture are in perfect harmony in their responses to the above questions. It is in this first Part that we turn to the history of the Roman Catholic church.

Preaching, praise and persecution

To understand Roman Catholicism and how it emerged we need to first look at the beginnings of the New Testament (NT) Church. It is in the book of "The Acts of the Apostles", in the Holy Bible, that we first see the activity and growth of the NT church. We note in Acts 2v41-47 what marked them out; *"they that gladly received his word were baptised...continued steadfastly in the apostle's doctrine and fellowship, and in breaking of bread, and in prayers...praising God"*. We also observe throughout the Book of Acts that the early church suffered much for their faith.[2] Throughout these times of preaching, praise and persecution the church grew phenomenally. This pattern would continue until the beginning of the fourth century.

However, something else was appearing: errors began to creep into the church. Ironically, certain errors came in because the church was trying to fight against false teaching and heresy. As soon as A.D. 115 it was taught in the works of Ignatius, bishop of Antioch, that the position of bishop was to be above all other offices. By A.D. 258, Cyprian of Carthage had taught that bishops could trace their line down to Peter and could mediate between the people and God. Perhaps you can see where this is all heading - the Papacy and Rome. But it was not the RC church as yet.

In the face of heresy and persecution, a stand had to be made by men of authority...

Why was this happening? By the end of the first century the first leaders of the church, the apostles were no longer alive, and many of their disciples were nearing old age. Secondly, the NT as we have it now had not been collated together in one canon - instead it consisted of the various books been read out in churches. It would not be until the fourth century when the NT would be brought together and the church would have the Bible within 'one cover'.[3] In the third place, we must remember that the church was in its earliest stages. "They did not stand where we stand today, with the help of twenty centuries of reflection on God's Word", but they stood at the beginning of the church's history, "and therefore at the beginning of theological thought".[4] On top of all this there was constant persecution. In the face of heresy and persecution, a stand had to be made by men of authority, and thus the elevation of bishops began.

A cross in the sky

Many have said that the RC church was born in the year 313. What is significant about this year? As already stated, the church was suffering persecution and had done since its birth. The source of this persecution was the pagan Roman Empire. There were a number of reasons for this persecution, but all stemming from the church's separation from the world's beliefs and lifestyles.[5]

By A.D. 312 the persecution had not abated and the Roman Empire still had no formidable rival in its world domination; but there was instability and disorder, and internal strife. Roman leaders and armies faced each other in battle; two men in particular vied for the position of power in Rome. In Rome was Maxentius and marching into Italy was Constantine with his army.

The day before the battle outside the city of Rome, it is said that in a vision Constantine saw the sign of a cross and above it the words 'In hoc signo vinces' - 'In this sign conquer'. The next day, October 28, 312, Constantine with his army advanced behind a man-made cross. They defeated Maxentius and his army and Constantine professed conversion to Christianity. Constantine was now supreme in the West. In A.D. 313 Constantine issued the Edict of Milan, which guaranteed freedom of religion to Christians.

Whether Constantine was truly converted is debatable; history records he would go on to murder members of his own family. What is more significant to this study, and which adds further doubt to his Christian profession, is his policy towards the enlargement of the church.

Constantine must have reasoned that rather than the empire being divided between pagans and Christians, why not fuse the two together. It was not the first and it would not be the last time that the error of *unity without truth* would be pursued.

Widening the door

Up to this time there had been persecution, due primarily to the church seeking to be biblically separate from the world and its pagan practices. But now Christianity became the state religion, and conversion became easy with 'former' pagans bringing in to the church their pagan ideas. The command of God that His people be holy (1 Peter 1v16), that is separate from the things of the world, was disregarded.

Although there had been error previously, persecution had helped purify the church from false believers and beliefs. With Constantine's peace and prosperity, came paganism; false teaching and practices began to multiply. Previously the worship was in *"spirit and in truth"* (John 4v23), but gradually it began to become aesthetic, man-made and worldly. When Constantinople was dedicated as the new Roman capital in A.D. 330, a half pagan and half Christian ceremonial was used. In time, Constantine would decide that he ruled the church, presiding over important meetings with bishops and church leaders. But Scripture speaks of the church's supreme spiritual rule belonging to only one, *that being Christ* (Isaiah 9v7; John 18v36-37).

From the time of Constantine, the church would reap the consequences of this compromise. He had 'widened the church's front door', and worldliness began to flood in. As we will see later, "the multiplication of holy days, the veneration of saints, martyrs, and relics, and the value of pilgrimages and holy places often pushed truly spiritual concerns into the background".[6] The RC Church as we know it today had not yet been visibly born, but it was in the state of conception. As well as paganism there was another factor that would bring about the birth of the RC Church on the world stage; it would be the rise of the papacy.

Five fathers

We have already seen that as early as A.D. 115 the position of bishop was being lifted above Scriptural warrant. The term 'bishop' no longer was synonymous with the terms 'elder', 'overseer' and 'pastor'.[7] Instead it meant the leading elder in a local church or the head of all the churches in a city. Cyprian, who was bishop of Carthage between the years 249-258, taught that the bishop was a kind of high priest mediator and had an apostolic succession from Peter, the first bishop of Rome! But history and Scripture speak of no such thing. At most it could be said that it is probable Peter died in Rome.

By the year 451, in five cities of the Roman empire the bishops were known as '*patriarchs*', from the Greek word meaning 'first (or ruling) father'. The five cities were Rome, Constantinople, Alexandria, Antioch and Jerusalem. Not only did they begin to exalt themselves over bishops in smaller churches but also there would be rivalry between themselves, particularly between Rome in the West and Constantinople in the East.

In taking on such a title as '*father*', in the context of church relationships, they had forgotten the words of the Lord Jesus in Matthew 23v8, "*call no man your father upon earth, for one is your Father, which is in heaven*". But, it was the patriarch in Rome who geographically held the most power. He was the head of the church for the whole of the West of the empire. And it was he alone who became known as the 'Pope', from the Latin word 'papa', meaning 'father'.

Bishop of Rome

It was in Rome that more and more power had been growing. Ever since Constantine had moved the capital of the Roman Empire to Byzantium (which he renamed Constantinople after himself) in the East, the main powerful figure left in Rome, in the West, was the pope. People now looked to him when issues had to be resolved. As various church controversies and disputes came to the fore, the influence of Rome and its bishop began to grow; it was the judgment of Rome, which would usually win the day. This was particularly felt following the fall of the Western Roman Empire in A.D. 476; the pope became the most influential person not just in Rome but Europe.

As early as A.D. 417, the bishop of Rome, Innocent I, wrote that final authority lay with Rome.[8] A further step was taken when Zosimus, Rome's next bishop, said no one had the right to question a decision taken by the Church of Rome. In A.D. 445, Leo, the bishop of Rome, asserted in his famous *Tome of Leo*, the title of 'Pope'. That same year, the Emperor Valentinian III emphasized the pre-eminence of Leo as Pope.[9] Claims began to be asserted that the apostle Peter was the first bishop of Rome. For 145 years,

> **...the influence of Rome and its bishop began to grow; it was the judgment of Rome which would usually win the day.**

the title of 'Pope' was argued, until in A.D. 590, Gregory the Great agreed that the title should stay. The bishop of Rome would be regarded as the Pope.

Was this the birth of the RC Church, as we know it today? Not quite, for Pope Gregory the Great stopped short of the heresy that is now found in the RC Church - that the pope is the 'Universal bishop' of the church and 'Vicar of Christ' (i.e. in place of Christ). When the patriarch of Constantinople, John IV, claimed the title of 'Universal bishop', Pope Gregory warned him that such a title was "blasphemous, anti-Christian and diabolical".[10]

It was in the 7th century following Gregory the Great that the RC church began to 'hatch out of her egg'. Boniface III, as pope in 607, had the Emperor Phocas confer on him the title of 'Universal bishop'. "It was at that point...this anti-Christian spirit began to manifest itself...From that date onwards the papacy grew in strength and Christian doctrine declined in force and clarity".[11]

But it was not just ecclesiastical authority but political and temporal authority that the pope began to assert. When in the year 800, Charlemagne (Charles the Great) became Holy Roman Emperor, it was the bishop of Rome, Pope Leo III, who crowned him. From that time on the popes believed they had the authority and power to enthrone and depose monarchs at their will.

The following years would see corrupt and wicked men opposing and murdering each other to attain the position of pope.[12]

Establishment of power

It was, however, in the eleventh century that the RC Church would emerge out of its shell in its full strength and heretical 'splendour'. The church in the East, with its centre in Constantinople, had never accepted the title of pope for the bishop of Rome, and never would. Differences in language, religious practice and doctrine drove the West and East apart, and it would be the rise of the papacy that finally drove in the wedge. The East rejected the papacy as the church's visible head and held that the five patriarchs should form the leadership for Christians. There were attempts to remove the differences, but these failed.

In the year 1054 (following certain political and military events between the two sides) the church finally split. In that year the 'Roman Catholic Church'[13] and the 'Greek Orthodox Church' were visibly born; the latter to this day not accepting the authority of the pope. Through *peace, prosperity, paganism and papal power* the RC Church made its official entry on to the world stage.

Ironically, both the Western and Eastern churches were very much alike. Both had been influenced by paganism; both now bore the marks of compromise and apostasy.

Both had raised up the position of their bishops beyond Scriptural warrant. Magnificent buildings were erected, with Constantine and his mother Helena leading the way, the finest being in Constantinople. Bishops had gold covered thrones and ornate and expensive vestments. "It was a period of pomp and pride, of sounding brass and tinkling cymbals, without spiritual reality".[14] Sadly, the ordinary people would be taken up more and more with the ceremony and beauty, without understanding their meaning. Truth and spirituality would be lost for outward show and falsehood.

By this time, in 1054, other signs of apostasy were present. Saints were being prayed to and images worshipped. The pagan belief that the dead could help the living was further seen in the worship of relics of dead saints. The mother of Constantine even claimed to have found the true cross on which Christ died. Mary, the mother of Jesus, began to stand out as the greatest of saints and became known as "the Queen of heaven". This would lead on to the 'phenomena' of Marian apparitions and shrines to Mary.

Within thirty years, the next bishop of Rome, Gregory VII (Hildebrand), would seal the power of the Papacy with his declarations. These included the following:

1. The bishop of Rome alone is universal bishop.

2. He alone can depose bishops or receive them again.

3. He alone has power to make new laws in the church.

4. All princes ought to kiss his foot.

5. No book is canonical (i.e. with authority) without his authority.

6. He is subject to no human judgment.

7. The Roman Church never did nor ever can err (i.e. be wrong in what it teaches).

Ceremonies, crusades and corruption

Slowly but surely the power and authority of God's Word was being replaced with the pseudo power of ceremonies and so called miracles. People's trust was no longer being directed to the one true Saviour found in the Scriptures but in the church itself with its popes and priests.

The belief that the bread and wine are changed during the mass (celebration of the Eucharist) into Christ's body and blood (transubstantiation) was generally believed. By the eleventh century, this had developed into the belief that the mass was an offering again of Christ's sacrifice for the sins of the living and the dead.

...the power and authority of God's Word was being replaced with the pseudo power of ceremonies...

In the year of 1095, the RC Church would preach that a man's sins would be washed away if he died fighting in the Crusades. Over a hundred years later, in 1227, Pope Innocent III began the feared 'inquisition', an organisation to uncover, physically punish and burn 'heretics'. Belief was no longer in spirit and truth, but by sword and fire.

Bereft of God's Spirit and drunk with worldly power, the corruption of the papacy continued. In 1378, infighting resulted in two rival popes, Urban VI and Clement VII. They were both elected separately by the church and each excommunicated the other! By 1409, there were three rival popes - Gregory XII, Benedict XIII and Alexander V! The inconsistency of the RC Church's claim that the pope had a direct line of succession from the apostle Peter was glaringly apparent.[15]

Men, ceremonies, traditions and methods were usurping the place of Christ and His Word.[16] The doctrine of faith only in Christ, and in His Word, had been pushed into the darkness.

Flames in the darkness

Had the true church disappeared? Was the truth lost? We find our answer not only in history but also in the Bible. Christ said, *"I will build my church and the gates of hell shall not prevail against it"* (Matthew 16v18; cf. Daniel 7v13-14).

Believers without and within the Church of Rome would form Christ's indestructible church.

Even before the darkness had begun to cover the Roman Church, there were flames burning brightly in other parts of Europe. Only brief snapshots are possible in this study.

In A.D. 432 a man who would become known as **Patrick** (385-461) arrived with others in Ireland. He was neither Irish nor under the authority of the Church of Rome.[17] Through his preaching and tireless work many were converted to Christ. By his death in 461, the Celtic church was established. From this church missionaries would go forth.

In the year 580, **Columban** set out with twelve assistants to what is now France, and then Switzerland. Previous to this, in 563, another Irish monk **Columba** (521-597) with twelve assistants had sailed to Scotland and founded a monastery in Iona from which they evangelised Scotland and the North of England. From Iona, **Aidan** (died 651) was sent to Lindisfarne, from where, with his fellow monks, he evangelised the kingdom of Northumbria. Though there was error in that they lived celibate and monastic lives, they were vigorously evangelistic knowing the spiritual reality of the life changing Gospel.

In time, however, the Celtic church was swallowed up into the Roman Church, largely through decisions made at the synod of Whitby in 664. As the RC Church began to descend into the darkness of apostasy, other flames began to blaze even more brightly.

Blazes of glory

In about 1170, **Peter Waldo** (or **Valdes**) a merchant of Lyons, France, came to understand there is one Mediator, that saints should not be worshipped and the *Scriptures alone* are the basis of faith. Soon he had a band of followers and founded a movement called the **Waldensians**. They visited southern France, Switzerland and northern Italy preaching the Word of God. For several centuries, they were persecuted and killed by the RC Church.

In fourteenth century England, a RC scholar and priest by the name of **John**

Wyclif(fe) (1330-1384) began to denounce the sale of indulgences,[18] masses for the dead and the worship of images and relics. He went on to attack the Roman doctrine of transubstantiation, organize an order of preachers (known as 'Lollards'), and translate the Bible from Latin into English so all could know the Truth. But after his death the RC church retaliated. Lollards were burnt as heretics, Wyclif's translation condemned, and his bones dug up and burnt.[19]

In Bohemia, Wyclif's writings influenced **John Huss** (1369-1414), a faithful student of God's Word. He became the preacher at a RC chapel in Prague, where "he exposed the…sins of the clergy, and fed the hungry with the bread of life."[20] For his faithfulness, Huss was excommunicated and in 1415, at the Council of Constance, condemned to burn as a heretic. His words just before his death capture the heart and mind of the many that would die before the fury of Rome: *"I am willing patiently and publicly to endure this dreadful, shameful and cruel death for the sake of thy gospel and the preaching of thy Word."*[21]

About eighty years later, in Florence, Italy, a RC monk, **Jerome Savonarola** (1452-1498), began to preach against the corruption in the church and the need for repentance of sin. The effect was that many were converted. But, it did not please the pope. Pope Alexander VI sought to bribe Savonarola, and when that failed had him belittled. Savonarola would eventually be tortured and then burned. His crime: preaching God's Truth.

These were only a few of the many who shone in the darkness. It was not until the next century that these scattered flames would join to cause such a blaze of truth in the RC Church, that the darkness would finally be dispelled from many hearts and nations.[22]

Protestation and separation: the Reformation

Whilst studying the book of Romans, **Martin Luther** (1483-1546), a German Augustinian monk, came to understand the reality of Paul's words, *"The just shall live by faith"* (Romans 1v17). *He realised his personal helplessness and inability to earn salvation through his good works.* In 1511, his eyes were further opened; when visiting Rome, he saw its wickedness and corruption. *But it was on October 31st, 1517, that 'the reformation' of the church began.* On that day,

Luther nailed to the door of the Castle Church of Wittenberg his 95 theses. These were 95 reasons or arguments against the sale of indulgences (see footnote 18) and explaining the nature of true repentance. Copied, printed and distributed, they were soon being read all over Europe.

Luther's public complaint "went to the heart of the existence of the [RC] Church"[23] (though he did not yet see it that way). God's grace in salvation could not be bought or earned, otherwise it would not be grace (Ephesians 2v8-9). Yet the whole RC system of sacraments was based on the principle that the church dispensed God's grace at a price. Pope Leo X soon realised the threat that Luther's protest had on his authority and the doctrine of the church, and he demanded that Luther recant. Luther did not recant but instead would go on and make his stand against Rome.

> ...the whole RC system of sacraments was based on the principle that the church dispensed God's grace at a price.

Whilst Luther blazed a trail of truth in Germany, other men would be raised by God to dispel the darkness throughout Europe. Men such as **Ulrich Zwingli** (1484-1531), a priest in Zurich, Switzerland, **John Knox** (1514-1572), also a priest, in Scotland and **John Calvin** (1509-1564) in Geneva, Switzerland. These men were all RCs who had hoped to reform Catholicism from within, but Rome would not change. *Their subsequent separation would become known as 'the Reformation'.*

England also would receive the light. One of the most significant reformers was **William Tyndale** (c. 1494-1536), a Hebrew and Greek scholar. Refused by the RC church to be allowed to translate the Scriptures from the original languages into English, he fled to the continent. There he translated the NT and most of the OT into English. He was finally betrayed and captured in Antwerp, and publicly strangled and burnt. But it was too late for the RC Church; *the English people had the Word of God in their hands.*

Five foundational doctrines

The crucial doctrinal issues of the Reformation were encapsulated in the 'slogans' coined by Luther: *sola gratia* (by grace alone), *sola Christi* (by Christ alone) *sola Scriptura* (by Scripture alone) and *sola fide* (by faith alone). This all pointed to salvation being *soli Deo gloria* (to God's glory alone).[24]   The "Reformers knew they could no longer remain within the Roman Catholic church...[and] were convinced that the Roman Church had departed from Biblical Christianity at these crucial points".[25]

The RC Church however, would not only continue with the fires of persecution but with what would become known as the Counter Reformation to reclaim hearts and minds. Pope Paul III called The Council of Trent (1545-1563) to counter the Reformation and reaffirm RC doctrines such as justification by faith *and works*, transubstantiation, purgatory and celibacy of clergy. The Inquisition was revived and men such as Ignatius Loyola and his Jesuit Order of priests used literally almost any means to win people back to Rome.

Although there was some success, the truth that the Reformation had brought had transformed hearts and minds, and men no longer wished to return to the darkness.

History of heresy

Has the RC church changed? Some would claim that things are different in the 21st century. However, if we take a brief look at the development of the Church's official doctrine, we see the rapid advance and not the repentant retreat of heresy.

600   Worship in Latin.

750   Temporal power of Pope

788   Worship of relics permitted.

850   Holy water.

1079 Celibacy (priests not allowed to marry).

1090 Rosary (repetitious praying with beads).

1190 Sale of indulgences (time in purgatory shortened if money given to church).

1215 Transubstantiation (bread and wine change to the literal body and blood of Christ).

1215 Confession of sins to priests.

1220 Adoration of the wafer (adoration of the 'body of Christ').

1229 Bible forbidden to laymen.

1274 Purgatory (place between heaven and hell where sins paid for).

1508 Prayer 'Ave Maria' (praying to Mary)

1545 Tradition given equal authority as Scripture (at the Council of Trent).

1546 Apocrypha given equal authority as Scripture (at the Council of Trent).

1854 Immaculate Conception of Mary (perfect at birth).

1870 Papal Infallibility (Pope perfect in what he decrees).

1922 Mary co-redeemer with Christ.

1950 Bodily Assumption of Virgin Mary (taken to heaven rather than face death).

This has continued apace to the present. Rather than refuting these doctrines and practices, which find no support in the Bible, the RC Church has reasserted them. Some recent examples highlight this.

In 2001, the arrival of St Theresa's bones in the Republic of Ireland caused crowds to flock and venerate them. The Times newspaper for Saturday December 14, 2002, reported that these same relics had been allowed into Baghdad, Iraq. On the verge of a possible war, the bones were to comfort the Iraqi RCs, *who kneel before them* and pray for peace.

A few years prior to this in 1998, Pope John Paul II (1978-2005) stated, "We define that the Holy Apostolic See and the Roman Pontiff has primacy over the whole world. And that the same Roman Pontiff is the successor of blessed Peter, Prince of the Apostles and true Vicar of Christ, head of the whole church and father and teacher of all Christians, and that upon him, in blessed Peter, our Lord Jesus Christ conferred the full power of shepherding, ruling and governing the universal church..."[26]

In May 2005, representatives of the RC church and the Anglican church published a document, *Mary: Hope and grace in Christ*. In essence, this

---

document affirmed that the RC beliefs in the immaculate conception and bodily assumption of Mary are "authentic expressions of Christian belief". It stated that, "we do not consider the practice of asking Mary and the saints to pray for us as communion-dividing" and private devotions inspired by apparitions of Mary are "acceptable".[27][28]

Relics, popes, saints and the exaltation of Mary continue to usurp and devalue the place of Christ and His Word. Rome with its sacramental method of salvation and its papal authority clearly has not changed.[29]

New clothes, no change

As we began this study, we cited a number of Christian organisations and people who regard the RC church as Christian. Some are saying that Rome is more conciliatory and open to change. But, if one was to examine some of the documents such as ECT and the joint declaration with the Lutherans, and as we have seen above, in the previous paragraphs, it is clear that Rome's doctrines have not changed.[30]

However, there have been certain events that have given the impression of remarkable change, if not in doctrine at least in practice; and this is not only in its policy towards Protestant/Evangelical churches. In 1964 Vatican Council II was convened and made certain declarations. In respect of Protestant churches it said, "It follows that the separated Churches…though we believe they suffer from… defects…have by no means deprived of significance and importance in the mystery of salvation".[31] What was more remarkable was that it also stated, "The plan of salvation includes those also who acknowledge the Creator; foremost among these are the *Muslims…*"[32] In 1986, Pope John Paul II convened a meeting in Assisi, Italy, where *160 leaders of different religions* prayed together. The pope said, "We will stand side by side asking God to give us peace".

Rome is seeking to legitimise itself and minimise opposition.

In 1999, an ecumenical meeting was held in Dallas, USA. This was attended by a Nigerian RC cardinal named Francis Arinze. When asked if one could be right with God while not believing in Jesus Christ, Arinze appealed to Vatican II, *"…God's grant of salvation includes not only Christians but Jews, Muslims,*

Hindus and people of good will." When asked "Can you still get to heaven without accepting Jesus?" he answered, "Expressly, yes!"[33]   It is significant that Arinze, prior to the death of Pope John Paul II in 2005, was regarded by many to be the next pope.

Twelve days after the terrorist attack of September 11th, 2001, Pope John Paul II declared before the predominantly Muslim nation of Kazakhstan, "...*This is a truth which Christians...share with Muslims: it is faith in the one God...*"[34]

What is it the RC Church doing? *The truth is that Rome has not changed; it has simply put on a new set of clothes.* Rome is seeking to legitimise itself and minimise opposition. Its line is that other movements and religions have some truth, but the ultimate truth belongs to the RC Church - it is the 'mother church' and its sacramental system of salvation remains.[35]

The doctrines of this ecclesiastical organization have not changed. In fact they are now adding new errors to the old ones

Serious warnings

We saw at the beginning of this study that men and movements appear already to have begun to fall into the lap of the 'mother church'. They have become anaesthetized to the deadly error of Rome, and appear enamoured by the fallacy of *unity without truth.*

One may ask whether they have forgotten the lessons of history. Do they not recall what first led the Roman church into the darkness, how that darkness enveloped the church and how the light of truth finally blazed forth in the 16th century?

This study began with serious questions and it closes with serious warnings:

"Some evangelicals today think that times have changed and that it is now possible to hold a dialogue and to collaborate with the Roman Catholic Church in order to achieve Christian unity. This is a deception of Satan. The doctrines of this ecclesiastical organization have not changed. In fact they are now adding new errors to the old ones and in particular they are working towards bringing in all the other religions...It is therefore of utmost importance for us at the present time to obey the exhortation of the Word of God, *"Be ye not unequally yoked together with unbelievers..."* (converted priest Salvatore Gargiulo).[36]

Another converted priest, Bartholomew F. Brewer, has written, *"The history of the Catholic church is the history of paganism, corruption and the lust for power. The church has not mellowed, and it should not be trusted."*[37]

The error of Rome is not new. The apostle Paul did not mince his words when he said: *"If any preach any other gospel unto you than ye have received, let him be accursed."* (Galatians 1v9). He knew the Gospel, and therefore the salvation of souls, was at stake. *Rome denies the truth of God's Word that Scripture alone is sufficient (2 Timothy 3v15-17), that justification is only by faith in Christ alone (Romans 3v28; Galatians 2v16) and that this faith comes only by God's grace (Ephesians 2v1-10).*

Either we put our trust in a system of sacraments and a fallible pope, or we place it in a sufficient Saviour and His perfect Word. Like the Waldensians, Wyclif, Huss, Luther, Tyndale, Calvin and the multitude of others we must make our stand against error and therefore apart from the RC Church. And like these past figures, in compassion, we must also warn those within the RC church of the spiritual danger they are in. Truth demands it. God's glory demands it. The eternal fate of souls demands it.

Soli Deo gloria.

"...the holy scriptures... able to make thee wise unto salvation through faith which is in Christ Jesus."
(2 Timothy 3v15)

"For by grace are ye saved through faith; and that not of yourselves; it is the gift of God: Not of works, lest any man should boast."
(Ephesians 2v8-9)

Part 2

Roman Catholic Doctrines

Roman Catholic Doctrines

In this second Part we examine Roman Catholic (RC) doctrine by asking ten questions. These questions address specific RC doctrines, with each question accompanied by brief Scriptural responses. A Bible will be needed - one is invited to use a RC Bible to check the Scripture references.

1. Was Peter the first pope?

The RC Church believes Peter was its foundation and head i.e. the first of many popes.

a. The RC Church primarily bases its belief on an interpretation of **Matthew 16v18**: *"Thou art Peter, and upon this rock I will build my church"*. They teach that Christ made Peter the foundation of the church. But the passage needs to be examined in context:-

> **i.** The Greek word for Peter is *"petros"* (masculine gender) = *"a little stone"*. The Greek word for rock is *"petra"* (feminine gender) = *"the rock"*.
>
> The Lord Jesus is speaking of two different things of which only one could be a foundation; one little stone and a "rock the size of Gibraltar" (Stuart Olyott)!
>
> **ii.** Christ would (five verses later) reprove Peter and call him Satan!

The person of Peter does not appear to be a stable foundation. See **Matthew 16v23**.

iii. In the context of the rest of Scripture it is *Christ* Who is the Rock that is the foundation of the Church *(Peter himself states this).* He is Messiah Who has come to begin His church. See **Isaiah 28v16; I Corinthians 3v11; 10v4; Ephesians 2v20; 1 Peter 2v5-8**.

iv. It is Christ and *Peter's testimony of Jesus Christ as the Messiah and Son of God*, with the teachings of the other apostles, which forms the foundation (rock) of the church. See **Matthew 16v16-18; Ephesians 2v20**.

The foundation has now been laid, and there is no more need for apostles i.e. *no need for succession*. What is needed is to build on the foundation (cf. **Ephesians 2v21-22**).

v. Not just Peter but all believers are given the keys of the kingdom i.e. we have the Gospel to tell that Jesus is the Christ and Son of God. We thus 'open' God's kingdom to unbelievers. See **Matthew 16v19; Matthew 18v18-19; John 20v23; Acts 2v38**.

Other important Scriptural truths:

b. Peter never called himself pope or bishop of Rome. Neither did he pass his office on to another i.e. there was no succession - **1 Peter 1v1; 5v1; 2 Peter 1v1**.

c. Peter was fallible and was rebuked by Paul - **Galatians 2v11-14**.

d. He was not above other apostles - **Acts 15 v1-29; Galatians 2v9; 2 Corinthians 12v11**.

e. Peter was married (unlike the pope) - **Matthew 18v4; 1 Corinthians 9v5**.

f. He would not allow anyone to bow down to him for he was but a man - **Acts 10v25-26**.

g. Christ is the head of the church not Peter - **Ephesians 5v23**.

h. We are not to call anyone 'father' ('pope') in the context of the church - **Matthew 23v8**.

i. Following Paul, no one can fulfill the criteria to be an apostle - **Acts 1v21, 22, 25; 1 Corinthians 15v8-9**.

2. Is Church tradition as authoritative as Scripture?

a. *Scripture alone* is sufficient for all matters of faith and conduct - **2 Timothy 3v15-17**.

b. We are warned not to add to Scripture - **Deuteronomy 4v2; Revelation 22v18-19**.

c. Jesus condemned the traditions of men - **Matthew 15v3,6,9; Mark 7v5-13**.

d. The "traditions" referred to by Paul are the teachings of him *as an apostle*, who with the other apostles laid the foundation of the church (see above)

- **2 Thessalonians 2v15; 3v6**. But, he condemned the traditions of men (**Colossians 2v8; Titus 1v14**).

e. Paul said to study and *"Preach the word"*, not church tradition - **2 Timothy 2v15; 4v2**.

f. All believers, by the Holy Spirit, can interpret the Scripture - **Acts 17v11; 1 John 2v27**.

g. Paul's teaching was tested by Scripture itself; so should church tradition - **Acts 17v11**.

N.B. The **Apocrypha** comprises of 15 books added to the O.T. by the RC Church. They are not found in the original Hebrew O.T., were never quoted from by Christ and it took almost 2000 years after the O.T. was completed for the RC Church to 'add' them (in 1546)!

We see that *Scripture alone* **is authoritative in teaching of Christ and of Christian living.**

3. Is the church to have priests?

His Title and Position

a. There is only one *high priest*, Jesus Christ - **Hebrews 7v17, 24-27.**

b. The O.T. priesthood passed away *when Christ offered Himself* as the sufficient and final sacrifice for sins - **Hebrews 10v12-14.**

c. Church officers are never described as 'priests' in N.T. - **Acts 20v17; 1 Timothy 3v1.**

d. All believers are priests in that they have direct access to God through Christ - **1 Peter 2v5-9; Revelation 1v5-6** (cf. **Hebrews 10v19-20**).

His Celibacy

a. Not only are church ministers *allowed to marry*, but also it is beneficial as ability to rule one's children well demonstrates one's aptitude to rule the church - **1 Timothy 3v2-5.**

b. The O.T. priests, as well as the apostles, were married - **Leviticus 21v31.**

c. The apostle Paul said, *"it is better to marry than to burn"* with lust - **1 Corinthians 7v9.**

His Confessional

a. Only God can forgive sin. To him alone we must pray - **Mark 2v5-11; Acts 8v22.**

b. If we sin, there is only one advocate with God, that is, Jesus Christ - **1 John 2v1.**

c. All believers are able to say, "Your sins are forgiven if you believe on Christ" and by the same token say, "Your sins are retained if you do not believe" - **John 20v23.**

d. We share our burdens with other believers, not confess to 'priests' - **James 5v16.** *"When Peter sinned, he confessed to God and was forgiven; when Judas sinned, he confessed to a group of priests and committed suicide!* (Matt. 27v3-5)" (Ralph Woodrow).

---

4. Is the sacrifice of the mass necessary?

Changing bread and wine into Christ's body and blood

a. When Christ performed a miracle such as the water into wine, there was a visible physical change - **John 2v8-10**. But in the mass nothing visibly changes!

b. Christ spoke of 'bread' *after* speaking of it as His 'body'. He was clearly speaking symbolically, as He did when He spoke of being *the door* and *the vine* - **1 Corinthians 11v24-26**.

c. To 'partake' of Christ is not to eat Him physically but to believe on Him - **John 6v29-35**.

d. Bowing before the bread is idolatry as it is bread not the Son of God - **Exodus 20v4-5**.

Offering Christ as a sacrifice for sins of the living and dead

a. Daily offerings (of masses) cannot take away sin - **Hebrews 10v11**.

b. Christ offered one sacrifice for sins once and forever, never to be repeated. God's Word clearly says that *"there is no more offering for sin"* - **Hebrews 9v12,26; 10v12,18**.

c. Jesus' *final* words on the cross were, *"It is finished"* - **John 19v30**. Was He mistaken?!

d. Christ's resurrection *demonstrated* that man was justified before God - **Romans 4v25**.

e. Christ was *satisfied* that His work was done - **Isaiah 53v11** (cf. **Hebrews 10v17-18**).

f. Satisfied with His work He sat down on the right hand of God. Christ is now in heaven, not in a wafer - **Ephesians 1v20; Hebrews 10v12** (cf. **Acts 1v9**).

g. Christ's sacrifice *is final* and *sufficient* salvation for all His people - **Hebrews 10v14**.

h. Partaking of the bread and wine is observed in *remembrance* and as a *proclamation* of Christ's death, not as an offering up again of His life - **1 Corinthians 11v24-26**.

5. Do we go to purgatory to suffer when we die?

a. Jesus said believers in Him pass from death to life with *no condemnation* - **John 5v24**.

b. The dying thief was promised *paradise* that day *not purgatory* - **Luke 23v39-43**.

c. God's children go straight to be with Christ - **Philippians 1v23** (cf. **Luke 18v19-31**).

d. Christ has endured *all the suffering* necessary for sin - **Hebrews 10v12,17**.

e. Those who die in the Lord *rest* and are *blessed* - **Revelation 14v13**. ('Resting' and 'blessedness' are clearly not descriptions of man's state in purgatory!).

Purgatory passages?

The following Scriptural references are the few that are used to try to prove the doctrine of purgatory. Each reference is followed with the most appropriate Biblical explanation.

a. **1 Corinthians 3v8-15** - This speaks of the responsibility of ministers to do their work well.

b. **1 Peter 3v19** - The "disobedient" are the unbelieving people that Christ preached to through Noah. (see v20)

c. **Matthew 5v21-26** - If you die with no heart change you will not escape *hell's prison*.

What is clearly apparent, is that purgatory is not mentioned in any of the above scriptures.

6. Is Mary to be honoured as special?

Her immaculate conception (conceived without sin)

a. Mary "rejoiced in God *my Saviour*". Clearly, she needed saving from sin - **Luke 1v47**.

b. Mary needed to offer a sacrifice *for purification* after Christ's birth - **Luke 2v22-24**.

c. Mary erred in her understanding - **Luke 2v48-50**.

d. Christ put the Word of God and those who obeyed it before Mary - **Luke 11v27-28**.

e. The Bible is clear when it says *all* have sinned - **Romans 3v23**.

Her perpetual virginity

a. Joseph abstained from relations with Mary only *before* Christ's birth - **Matthew 1v25**.

b. Jesus is described as Mary's *"firstborn"*, i.e. she had other children - **Luke 2v7**.

c. Our Lord had brothers and sisters - **Mark 6v3**.

d. There is no indication that Mary disobeyed God's will for marriage - **Genesis 1v28**.

Her bodily assumption (taken to heaven without death)

God's Word speaks *only* of *Enoch* and *Elijah* who did not see death. There is no scripture or reason to say the same of Mary - **Genesis 5v21-24; 2 Kings 2v11**.

Her redeeming and mediatorial work (with Christ)

a. Jesus did not always heed His earthly mother's requests - **Matthew 12v46-50**.

b. Christ rebuked Mary when she made a request of Him - **John 2v4**.

c. The Lord instructed His disciples to pray, not to Mary, but *"Our Father"* - **Matthew 6v9**.

d. Jesus told sinners, *"Come unto me…"* ; He did not say, "Go to Mary" - **Matthew 28v11**.

e. The Bible says there is only *one* mediator - **1 Timothy 2v5**. If God tells us there is only one, there cannot

be two. (In any case, how can a sinful woman mediate for sinners?).

f. Is Mary our advocate when we sin? The scripture tells us it is Christ - **1 John 1v1-2**.

Her special veneration

a. We notice the wise men worshipped the Lord Jesus, not Mary - **Matthew 2v11**.

b. Mary is never referred to as 'mother of God'. She was the mother of Christ's human nature, but *not of His divine nature*, which existed from all eternity - **John 1v1-3,14; 8v57-58**.

c. Christ commanded *John alone* to take in Mary as his mother - **John 19v25-27**.

d. Christ said man is to worship and serve *only* God - **Matthew 4v10**.

e. If we are to 'honour' Mary let us heed her words to *obey Christ's words* - **John 2v5**.

7. Are we to venerate statues and pray to saints?

Statues

a. We are not to make any kind of image *and* bow down or serve it - **Exodus 20v4-6**. (This is the 2nd Commandment, but the RC Church

has absorbed the verses into the 1st Commandment, and split the 10th Commandment into two, making it the 9th and 10th!)

b. God purposefully did not appear

---

to His people, when He gave the Ten Commandments - **Deuteronomy 4v15-29**. Why? So that they would not make an image of Him.

c. God praised King Hezekiah for destroying a brass serpent He had commanded Moses to make, for the people had begun to venerate it - **2 Kings 18v3-4**.

d. The N.T. forbids making any image for worship - **Acts 17v16,29; Revelation 9v20**.

e. It is not statues, but God alone, we must trust - **Psalm 115v4-9; Isaiah 46v6-7**.

Saints

a. "Saint" was used in the plural to refer to ordinary Christians - **Ephesians 3v18; 5v3**.

b. "Saint" means *holy one*. "Holy" or "sanctified" means 'set apart' - set apart by Christ's sacrifice from a life of sin and set apart to God - **1 Corinthians 1v2; Hebrews 10v10**. All who believe in Christ are so set apart.

c. Both Peter and Paul did not allow men to bow before them - **Acts 10v25-26; 14v13-15**.

d. Paul said he could only help believers *whilst alive* - **Philippians 1v23-26**.

e. We are to ask in prayer of *God the Father* not of saints - **Matthew 7v7-11**.

f. God knows and loves His people; it is on Him we are to cast our cares - **1 Peter 5v7**.

g. When we come to the Father, we are to come *in Jesus' name alone* - **John 15v16**.

h. We do not need saints, when we have Christ who sympathizes with us and is *"touched with the feeling of our infirmities"* - **Hebrews 4v15-16**.

We see in addressing questions 3-7 that salvation and security rests in the work of *Christ alone*.

8. Is salvation through the church and its sacramental system or is it by God's grace alone?

The RC Church believes that salvation is attained through obedience to the church:

1. Man is born in 'original sin' = because of Adam's sin man is 'damaged' and not righteous, but

he still has the *will* to reach out to God.

2. *Baptism* (1st sacrament) cleanses man of original sin and infuses into the person grace making him spiritually 'alive'.

3. Christ's death 'opens the door' so that salvation can be possible for all man. "Christ has done his part, now we have to *cooperate* by doing ours."

4. The grace purchased by Christ's death, can only be received through the sacraments.

Man keeps sinning so keeping the rest of the *sacraments* cleanses the person. Man also has to do *good works* to build up the merit to get to heaven.

5. After death, just to make sure, the RC goes to *purgatory* to suffer and pay for any sins that haven't been forgiven. (Indulgences can be bought to shorten time in purgatory). Even after all that, the RC *cannot be sure* that he will enter heaven.

This whole system empowers the church and elevates man's pride. *Assurance is based upon what man can do;* God has been sidelined as just a participant.

But the Bible tells us that salvation is *all of God's grace.* It has to be because of the *depth and severity of sin* in man, and only God's grace will do.

1. Man is born in 'original sin' = because of Adam's sin man fell in totality. He is *dead* in sin, and like Lazarus in the tomb, cannot raise himself. He does not have the will to reach out to God, for his *will lies in bondage.* There is nothing in man to deserve heaven.

See **Genesis 2v17; Psalm 51v5; Romans 3v1-12; 5v12; 1 Corinthians 2v14.**

2. Man's remedy lies outside of himself for there is nothing he can do. *One greater than man has to break the chains and raise the dead.* God, therefore, elects a people not because of their will power or 'good' works (for they are of no avail) but *because of His mercy* - His undeserved favour.

See **John 15v16; Acts 13v48; Romans 9v15,16; Ephesians 1v4-5.**

3. Christ's death *effectually* saves those that God has chosen and given to His Son. Christ pays the debt, purchases a people and

imputes (puts to their account) His own righteousness to them. It is a *complete* and *finished* work that needs no repeating.

Christ's death did not 'open a door', rather Christ is the door. *He purchased a people not a possibility.*

See **Isaiah 53v11; John 17v9,19; 19v30; Romans 4v25; Ephesians 5v25.**

4. On the basis of Christ's death and righteousness, and not man's own works, God *regenerates* His chosen people. We do not have the strength to save ourselves, nor the willingness to believe. But, God *changes our sinful nature*, so that we are willing to believe.

See **John 3v7-8; 6v37,44; Acts 16v14; Ephesians 2v1-10; Titus 3v5-6.**

5. Those God has elected, purchased and called, He will *keep unto glory.* To say otherwise, would mean that God's plan of salvation has failed.

See **John 6v39; 10v28-29; 17v1-2,15,22; Romans 8v1,28-39; Ephesians 1v13-14.**

In addition, we may say that true believers because they have been purchased by Christ's blood and sealed by the Spirit, *will* persevere unto the end.

See **John 15v16; Romans 8v3-4, 14; Ephesians 2v10; 1 Peter 2v9.**

We can be assured that if we have the Son, we have eternal life (1 John 5v12). In all this, there is no place for man's work. It is all of God and to His glory alone.

"Christ did not come to die to set up a system of meriting salvation as though His death relaxed the divine requirements for payment of sins committed. Neither did He die in hope that some one might believe through the exercise of their "self willed" will! No, He died to save an army of the lost. He died to guarantee the salvation of all those whom the Father would give to Him."

(Robert M. Zins; theologian, apologist, former Roman Catholic).

We see from this that salvation is of God's *grace alone,* in *Christ alone,* and thus to *God's glory alone.*

9. Is justification by faith and works or by faith alone?

Rome states *"If anyone says that the sinner is justified by faith alone...let him be anathema."*

The Bible states *"...a man is justified by faith without the deeds of the law."* (Romans 3v28).

The Meaning of Justification

Justification is concerned with a person's standing with God - it is *being made right with God.*

Rome teaches it is a *lifelong process of* being *made righteous.*

(Rome confuses and combines 'justification' and 'sanctification' together).

The Bible teaches that it is a *once-and-for-all act* of being *declared/reckoned righteous.*

Throughout the O.T. and the N.T. this declarative/judicial usage regarding justification is the most frequent and can be seen in the following examples:

a. Deuteronomy 25v1
To condemn = *declare* guilty.
To justify = *declare* not guilty.

b. Proverbs 17v15 - Justify means to *declare* acquitted/righteous, rather than to *make* righteous..

c. Luke 7v29 - Clearly the people cannot *make* God righteous - they are *declaring* it.

d. Luke 18v9-14 - The tax collector was not righteous in himself and yet was justified. ie God declared it.

e. Romans 5v16 - The contrast here as in the O.T. is "condemnation" with "justification".

In Adam we are *declared* sinful/guilty, but in Christ we are *declared* righteous/ not guilty. Justification is not about being made internally righteous but being declared righteous. How can that be; on what basis? We see on what ground next.

The Ground of Justification

Rome teaches that it is grounded on Christ *and the obedience of the sinner.*

The Bible teaches it is grounded only on *the obedience of Christ and His sacrificial death:*

a. No man is justified by his works or righteousness - **Romans 10v3-4; Galatians 2v16.**

b. Justification lies outside ourselves - only by God's grace - **Romans 3v24; Titus 3v7.**

c. *Christ* is the only basis of our

justification - **Acts 13v39;
I Corinthians 6v11.**

d. Christ and His obedience/ righteousness is the ground - **Romans 5v17-19.**

e. Also by Christ's death are we justified - **Romans 3v24-25; 5v9.**

f. A great exchange takes place. Our sin is imputed/reckoned to Christ, and His righteousness is imputed/ reckoned to us - **Romans 4v6-11; 2 Corinthians 5v21.**

Thus God looks on the sinner and declares him not guilty *in Christ's righteousness* and forgiven.

The Instrument of Justification
(ie How do we receive justification?)

Rome teaches *it comes through faith plus the sacraments and works.*

The Bible teaches it comes *only through faith* (faith being distinguished

from works) : **Romans 3v28; 4v5-6; Galatians 3v10-11; Philippians 3v9.**

This faith is a gift of God: **Ephesians 2v8-9; Philippians 1v29.**

Justification and Works

Rome teaches *works come before justification.*

The Bible teaches *works come after justification.* They are the fruit not the root:

Romans 3v31; 8v3-4; Titus 3v4-8; James 2v14-26

(Please note that James is dealing with false faith. Faith is not a "lonely faith", but it has works that follow. When Abraham was to sacrifice Isaac, he had already being justified!).

We see that justification is by *faith alone* in *Christ alone.*

10. Are we to believe that the pope is not the anti-christ?

Rome teaches that *the antichrist is yet to come.* There are Christians, however, who believe certain scriptures point to the office of pope as 'the antichrist'. The word "antichrist" can mean *'against'* or/and *'instead of'* [in place of] Christ. What

is clear is that in the RC Church we see 'priests', 'saints', Mary, and man's works *taking the place of Christ.* Above all, we see the pope not only presiding over this 'antichrist' system but also *calling himself:*

- *The church's foundation* (i.e. Peter) - but Christ is the foundation (**1 Corinthians 3v11**).

- *Head of the church* - but Christ is the head of the church (**Ephesians 5v23**).

- *Supreme shepherd* - but Christ is the Chief Shepherd (**1 Peter 5v4**).

- *Father of all Christians* - but there is only One Father (**Matthew 23v8**) and only Christ was prophesied as everlasting Father (**Isaiah 9v6**).

- *Infallible in his decrees* - but Christ was the only infallible teacher and man (**1 Peter 2v22**).

- *Judge of all men* - but Christ is the One Who will judge (**2 Corinthians 5v10**).

- *"Vicar (substitute) of Christ" = "I am God on the earth"* - no comment is needed!

We see the pope is 'antichrist' in the sense that he has claimed Christ's place for himself!

"...they have a zeal of God, but not according to knowledge.
For they being ignorant of God's righteousness,
and going about to establish their own righteousness,
have not subjected themselves unto the righteousness of God.
For Christ is the end of the law for righteousness
to every one that believeth."
(Romans 10v2-4)

Some Recommended Resources

Richard Bennett and Martin Buckingham, eds., *Far from Rome, Near to God - The Testimonies of Fifty Converted Roman Catholic Priests* (Edinburgh/Carlisle, Pennsylvania: The Banner of Truth Trust, 1997).*

Kirsten Birkett, *The Essence of the Reformation* (Sydney/London: Matthias Media, 1998).

Thomas F. Heinze, *Answers to my Catholic Friends* (Chino, CA: Chick Publications, 1996).

S.M. Houghton, *Sketches of Church History* (Edinburgh/Carlisle, Pennysylvania: The Banner of Truth Trust, 1980).

James G. McCarthy, *The Gospel According to Rome* (Eugene, Oregon: Harvest House Publishers, 1995).

James G. McCarthy, *Catholicism: Crisis of Faith* - video (Lumen Productions, 1991).

Oswald J. Smith, *The Catholic Bible Has The Answer* (B. McCall Barbour tract).

James R. White, *The God Who Justifies* (South Bloomington, Minnesota: Bethany House, 2001)

* This book has been translated from the English into German, Italian, Korean, Polish, Romanian and Spanish. Copies can be obtained by writing to Martin Buckingham at 68 Farmway, Braunstone, Leicester LE3 2XA.

Notes

[1] For instance John Stott affirmed with 2000 Evangelical Anglicans, in the Nottingham Congress Statement of 1977, "Seeing ourselves and Roman Catholics as fellow Christians we repent of attitudes that seem to deny it...We believe...visible unity...should be our goal", cited in Iain H. Murray, *Evangelicalism Divided - A Record of Crucial Change in the Years 1950 to 2000* (Edinburgh/Carlisle, Pennsylvania: The Banner of Truth Trust, 2000), p216. Billy Graham said (in Notre Dame), "I have no quarrel with the Catholic Church" and "I don't think the differences are important as far as personal salvation is concerned", cited in Murray, *Evangelicalism Divided*, p68. J.I. Packer in defending himself and the RCs and Evangelicals who signed the ECT document reasoned, "Those who love the Lord must stand together", cited in Murray, *Evangelicalism Divided*, p223.

[2] ACTS, 4v21; 5v40-41; 7v54-8v1; 9v1; 9v23; 12v1-4; 14v1-5,19; 16v19-24; 17v5-9; 19v29; 21v27-31

[3] Athanasius in 367 and the Synods of Hippo Regis (393) and Carthage (397) made official the canon of the NT. They in reality confirmed what had long been accepted by the church - the books of the NT.

[4] Harry R Boer, *A Short History of the Early Church* (Grand Rapids, Michigan: Eerdmans, 1995), p35.

[5] See for instance Richard Alderson, *The Early Christians - a taster* (Kent: Day One Publications, 1997), p23; Boer, *A Short History*, p45; John Foxe, *Foxe's Book of Martyrs - Popular Edition* ed. W. Grinton Berry (London: The Religious Tract Society), p17 and S.M. Houghton, *Sketches of Church History* (Edinburgh/Carlisle, Pennsylvania: The Banner of Truth Trust, 1980), p12 for more details.

[6] Boer, *A Short History*, p142.

[7] These terms, along with the term 'bishop', are used synonymously in the Holy Bible to describe the role of those who are the spiritual shepherds and leaders of each church; see Acts 14v23; 20v28; 21v18; Ephesians 4v11; Philippians 1v1; 1 Timothy 3v1-7; Titus 1v5-9; Hebrews 13v7,17. Though leaders and guides they were never to be regarded as 'above' any other believer - 1 Peter 5v14.

[8] Henry Bettenson, *Documents of the Christian Church* (London: Oxford University Press, 1975), p81.

[9] Ibid, p22.

[10] Maurice Roberts, *Christ and Antichrist* - audio (Salisbury Conference recordings, 2001), Session 3.

[11] Ibid.

[12] Two examples will suffice: Pope John XII (955-963) was charged by a Roman Synod with almost every crime that man is capable of, describing him as a monster of iniquity. Pope Boniface VIII put his predecessor to death by strangulation in 974, and was described by a Synod as 'a papal monster, who in his abject depravity exceeds all mortals' (cited in Houghton, *Sketches*, p51).

[13] The word 'Catholic' means "general, universal" and was used as early as the 2nd century to describe the orthodox Christian church. It was not initially a controversial term, however, Rome claimed the title, and it has stuck.

[14] Houghton, *Sketches*, p33. "The architects, musicians, artists, designers of furniture, vestments, and metalware, the composers of liturgies - all these now found means to express their faith not only spiritually but outwardly, with appeal, to eye, ear, and imagination." (Boer, *A Short History*, p141).

[15] Despite history's record of corrupt, murderous and opposing popes, one RC cardinal was able to say, before the conclave of clergy elected Cardinal Joseph Ratzinger (becoming Benedict XVI) as the 265th pope in 2005, "The Holy Spirit always ensures the right pope for the times. It did so in the case of John Paul II, and will do so again". Richard Owen, "To do list: defend the faith, unite the world" in *The Times*, No 68366, (Wednesday April 20 2005), p7.

[16] "Rome's theology revolves around her view of the magisterial power of the pope and the bishops…grace can reach sinners through the sacraments which only consecrated priests have the power to administer…The effect of this is to produce a gospel of works…" Alan Cairns, *Dictionary of Theological Terms* (Belfast/Greenville, South Carolina: Ambassador-Emerald International, 1998), p315.

[17] Patrick, when only a boy, was captured and taken from his home (British mainland) and sold as a slave in Ireland. Whilst a slave in Ireland, he was converted and subsequently escaped. But his heart lay with the Irish people and their need for the Gospel and thus he returned with its life giving message.

[18] Indulgences were pardons from purgatory. This was a place, taught by the RC Church, where souls suffered after death to 'pay off' some of the punishment for their sins. In effect this meant that a person could buy his way out of sin. (This, like many of the RC teachings, such as transubstantiation, clearly flies in the face of the truth that Christ has once and for all paid for sin on the cross and demonstrated this through his resurrection. See Holy Bible, John 19v30; Romans 4v25; Hebrews 7v27;9v28 - the sinner can add nothing to this but trust only in what Christ has done).

[19] This was by order of the Council of Constance in 1415. (Wyclif would become known

as 'The Morning Star of the Reformation').

[20] Houghton, *Sketches*, p69.

[21] Cited in Houghton, *Sketches*, p70.

[22] Chapter VI of J.H. Merle d'Aubigné, *History of the Reformation of the Sixteenth Century Vol. 1* (Edinburgh: Oliver & Boyd, 1846) contains fascinating accounts of various people in the RC Church who knew the truth of trusting in Christ alone for salvation during the period of darkness before the shining of the light of the Reformation. (All five volumes of d'Aubigné's History are available in one paperback volume published by Hartland Publications).

[23] Kirsten Birkett, *The Essence of the Reformation* (Sydney/London: Matthias Media, 1998), p42.

[24] Birkett in *The Essence of the Reformation* (p86-87) helpfully says, "In essence these Latin phrases were Luther's answers to four basic questions: **How can a person be right with God?** *Sola gratia* (by grace alone)...**How does this grace come?** *Sola Christi* (by Christ alone)...**How do we find Christ?** *Sola Scriptura* (by Scripture alone)...**What is our part?** *Sola fide* (by faith alone).

[25] Ibid, p88.

[26] *A Catechesis on the Church, Vol. 4, The Church Mystery Sacrament Community,* (1998, p275) as cited by Roberts, *Christ and Antichrist,* Session 1. Pope John Paul II was reaffirming a statement of the Council of Florence, 1439. The Catechesis has such chapter headings as 'The Pope Exercises Supreme Jursidiction', 'The Roman Pontiff is the Supreme Teacher' and 'The Successor Teaches Infallibly'. As Maurice Roberts points out, Pope John Paul II affirmed the "headship, supremacy and infallibility" of his position.

[27] Cited in Ruth Gledhill "Cracks in Anglican dissent over Mary" in *The Times,* No 68389, (Tuesday May 17 2005), p5. In the same article, Rev Rod Thomas, an evangelical and member of the Reform Conservative grouping, pointed out, "If Mary has been wholly and completely assumed into Heaven and we are able to pray to her, it goes completely against the grain of Jesus Christ being our great high priest who intercedes on our behalf with the Father".

[28] An excellent critique of the Marian apparitions and doctrines is Timothy F. Kauffman's *Quite Contrary - A Biblical Reconsideration of the Apparitions of Mary* (Huntsville, Alabama: White Horse Publications, 1994).

[29] Robert M. Zins states, "The Roman religion is based 100% on the notion that Jesus Christ came and left His own with an elaborate system. These religious rituals are to be performed in hopes of achieving salvation. They are to be administered through the power of Catholic priests who, by virtue of the sacrament of holy orders, take Catholic initiates through the sacraments. These sacraments are administered from the cradle to

the grave". *Romanism - The Relentless Roman Catholic Assault on the Gospel of Jesus Christ* (Huntsville, Alabama: White Horse Publications, 1995), p13.

[30] In regard to the Lutheran joint declaration W. Robert Godfrey comments: "In the affirmation of merit, the silence on imputation, the confusion of justification with renewal, and the use of 'imparting' as a functional equivalent for 'infusion', the real nature of the Joint Declaration is revealed. *The Roman Catholic position has not changed at all...The Lutherans alone have changed. They have abandoned the Reformation and betrayed the gospel".* "The Lutheran-Roman Catholic Joint Declaration" in *Banner of Truth*, Issue 436, (January 2000), p20. (Italics mine).

[31] *Vatican Council II, Vol II*, Austin Flanery, gen. ed., (Costello Publishing Company, 1992, p456), cited in Zins, *Romanism*, p198.

[32] *Vatican Council II, Vol II*, p367 cited in Zins, Romanism, p233.

[33] *Dallas Morning News*, Saturday March 20th, 1999, cited in Robert M. Zins, "Wrong At Both Ends: The need to re-think our apologetics with Rome today" in *CRN newsletter*, No 16, (2002), p3-4.

[34] See Richard Bennett and Robert J. Nicholson, "Islam and the Vatican - A new partnership with Muslims" in *Evangelical Times*, March 2002, (p30) & "Islam and the Vatican - Emotional Unity and its consequences" in *Evangelical Times*, April 2002, (p29) for more details. Bennett and Nicholson point out that the present pope contradicts previous popes who condemned Muslims and fought them in the crusades. By implication the crusading popes were 'wrong' and therefore heretics.

[35] Vatican II stated, "...the separated churches...derive their efficacy from the very fullness of grace and truth entrusted to the Catholic Church." (*Vatican Council II, Vol II*, p456), cited by Zins, *Romanism*, p198.

[36] Richard Bennett and Martin Buckingham, compilers, *Far from Rome, Near to God - The Testimonies of 50 Converted Catholic Priests* (Lafayette, IN: Associated Publishers & Authors, Inc., 1994), p81. Zins (*Romanism*, p208) states, *"Rome's courting of the pagan religions of this age will ultimately bring about the destruction of Romanism or a powerful one-world religious force. Either way, the current status of Rome keeps it strictly out of bounds for the Christian."*

[37] Bartholomew F. Brewer with Alfred W. Furrell, *Pilgrimage from Rome* (Greenville, South Carolina: Bob Jones University Press, 1986), p129.

Acknowledgements

I would like to place on record my indebtedness to Joe Hutton and the late Fred Harper for their enthusiasm for my original articles on Roman Catholicism, particularly Fred for his encouragement in printing them in his church magazine; Wallace Thompson for directing and encouraging the publication of this booklet and Melanie Dixey for her work in designing the booklet.